The North American INDIANS

The Marshall Cavendish illustrated history of

The North American INDIANS

Art and Totems

MARSHALL CAVENDISH
New York • London • Toronto • Sydney

Library Edition Published 1991

© Marshall Cavendish Limited 1991
© Pemberton Press Limited 1991

Published by Marshall Cavendish Corporation
2415 Jerusalem Avenue
Bellmore
N.Y. 11710

Series created by Graham Beehag Books
Produced by Pemberton Press Limited

Designed by Graham Beehag
Illustrated by Kerry Bridge
Edited by Maggi McCormick

Library of Congress Cataloging-in Publication Data

Oakley, Ruth,
  The Marshall Cavendish illustrated history of the North American
  Indians / Ruth Ena Oakley. – Limited ed.
      p. cm.
   Contents: v.1, In the beginning – v.2, Homes, food and clothing – v.3,
  A way of life – v.4, Religion and customs – v.5, Art and totems
  – v.6, Conflict of cultures.
      ISBN 1-85435-137-0 (set)
   1. Indians of North America – Juvenile literature. [1. Indians of
  North America.] I. Marshall Cavendish Corporation. II. Title.
  E77.4.O18 1990
  970.004'97–dc20   89-17371
                                                          CIP
                                                          AC

Printed and bound in the United States by Lake Book Manufacturing Inc.

Contents

Art and religion

For the native American, art was not just something to give him pleasure and satisfaction. When a wife carefully embroidered a shirt for her husband, it was not simply to please him or make him look good. The designs which the Indians used had deep and important religious meaning for them. Everything in the Indian's world had a spirit or power. He believed that power could be transferred to him by painting a picture on his tepee or sewing a symbolic design on his cloak.

Because it was the inner spirit of an animal or object that the artist was trying to capture, Indian art does not aim to produce an accurate physical likeness. When he decorated a tepee with a scene depicting a buffalo hunt, an Indian tried to capture the essence of the beasts. He was not aiming to produce a photographic representation of the animals' physical shape. Nor was he trying to paint an abstract impression of what the hunt was like.

Because this idea is unfamiliar to Westerners,

This Athapaskan buckskin shirt demonstrates the way in which Indians adapted new designs and methods of decoration learned from explorers and traders. The use of fringing and decorated panels is traditional; the floral embroidery shows a European influence.

A proud brave from Southeastern Idaho models similarly fringed and richly embroidered garments.

The Indians loved the bright red flannel which the British traders brought them. On this Haida tunic, the representation of a dogfish is appliqued in this fabric and outlined with white beads.

Indian art was at first thought to be simple and rather childish. As more was learned about Indian culture, Westerners realized that this view was a mistake.

If he was to survive, the Indian had to be observant and aware of his surroundings. He had to learn the ways of the animals; he had to know which plants were good to eat and which were poisonous; he had to be able to read the signs in the weather patterns. He had to notice detail.

From childhood, Indians were taught physical skills and how to make things, so that most of them were nimble with their hands. Perhaps for these reasons, most Indians seem to have been able to express their own artistic feelings. Art was not something which was left to a few experts. It was a part of life, and most of the everyday objects that an Indian used were well made and richly decorated.

Dance, drama, and masks

Dancing was an important part of Indian life. Often, dances were performed as part of a religious ceremony, but the Indians also enjoyed dancing as a social activity. When they were dancing ceremonially, they wore special costumes and masks. The masks were sometimes the heads of animals with extra decoration. Farming tribes such as the Iroquois made masks from the stalks and husks of corn. The Tlingits and other tribes of the British Columbia coast carved them from wood. They were sometimes made in the form of birds or animals, particularly hawks, bears, and beavers. Many represented human faces as well. All were richly decorated with paint, shell, copper, fur, deerskin, hair, or feathers.

Wampum was a kind of money made from shells which were strung into necklaces and belts. It was used by the Algonquin and Iroquois tribes of the northeast. The shells were generally white or purple clams and snails. Pieces from the column of the shell were held in a clamp and drilled with a pump drill to make them into beads which were sewn onto belts or threaded on strings. The purple beads were two or three times more valuable than the white.

The Dutch and English colonists manufactured wampum with metal tools and grindstones, and a wampum factory remained in use until World War I. Wampum was exchanged to seal agreements at tribal councils and offered as gifts to seal peace treaties and trade agreements.

Music

As an accompaniment to dancing, Indians sang, played drums, blew whistles, and shook rattles.

Among the eastern and southwestern tribes, rattles were made from dried gourds filled with pebbles or dried corn.

In the northwest, they were delicately and intricately carved from two pieces of wood. The pieces

This intricately carved shaman's wooden rattle is in the shape of a crane. On its back is the head of a goat, between whose horns sit two human figures.

There are many fine examples of the art of the eighteenth and nineteenth century Tlingit Indians in the Leningrad Museum of Anthropology and Ethnography. Carved and painted wooden masks, headdresses, pipes, bowls, and rattles; carved bone and horn; spruce-root hats, leather aprons, and blankets made from hair and vegetable fibers were taken home by Russian explorers and traders. From 1741 to 1867, Russia ruled Alaska, part of the Northwest Coast, and the Aleutian chain of islands. In 1867, Russia sold Alaska to the United States.

Right: A Plains Indian playing a skin drum.

were hollowed out, filled with pebbles, and bound together with threads of sinew or vegetable fiber on the handle. A shaman's rattle was usually round or oval and was used in healing ceremonies and dances. A chief's rattle was carved in the shape of a bird, usually a raven, with a human figure on its back. It was used when the chief spoke at a ceremony.

On the Plains, rattles were made by filling a wet rawhide bag with sand and molding it to the desired shape. When it dried, the sand was poured out. Pebbles were then put in and the opening at the neck plugged. The Iroquois made rattles from bark, turtle shell, and plaited basketry as well.

If a young brave of the Plains tribes wanted to tell a girl he wished to marry her, he played tunes on a flute outside her tepee at night.

Playing drums and singing to ask the gods for a good tobacco harvest.

Stories, myths, and legends

There were no books to read or televisions to watch during the winter evenings. The Indians entertained each other by telling stories. The wise old men of the tribe passed on to the children the stories they had heard when they were young. Stories about the mischievous god, Old Man Coyote; the creator god, Nanabozho, who took the form of a hare; the conceited Raven who was painted black for his pains; and the mighty Thunderbird.

A raven is painted on this Tlingit armor made of doubled layers of tanned hide. The parts of its body are painted flattened out in the Indian style.

Some of these stories provided ways of explaining the mysteries of life, like how the world began, what happens to us when we die, and why some people suffer tragedies through no fault of their own. Others taught children the virtues of courage, respect for elders, generosity, and honesty. The stories were made amusing, and the storytellers had the gift of painting pictures in the mind with words.

The Hopi Indians still make Kachina dolls as a memory aid for children to learn the names and special characteristics of their 250 deities. The dolls are carved from the roots of the cottonwood tree. The limbs, head, and weapons are carved separately and then glued to the body. They are then painted with bright poster paint on top of a white undercoat of kaolin. Decorations of colored feathers provide the finishing touches.

Wood carving

The men of the coastal tribes of British Columbia show particular skill in carving wood. Their masks and rattles have already been described in the sections on Dance and Music. They carved and decorated practically everything they used.

A carved and painted wooden chest, typical of the coastal tribes of British Columbia.

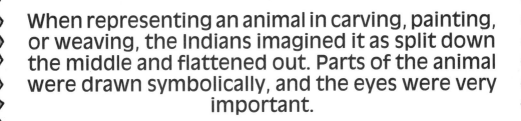

When representing an animal in carving, painting, or weaving, the Indians imagined it as split down the middle and flattened out. Parts of the animal were drawn symbolically, and the eyes were very important.

When they went to war, their armor, helmets, and visors were carved, painted, and decorated with shell. Many helmets had integral masks on them, carved out of the same piece of wood. The decoration included a representation of the tribe's totem, or special spirit. Specialists made carved decorations for the prows of canoes just as old-fashioned sailing ships had figureheads.

Houses, storage chests, dishes, bowls and spoons, pipes, combs, necklaces, and fish hooks all presented opportunities to display their skill. Some of their dishes in the form of animals such as beavers and

A carved and painted wooden chest, belonging to a Tlingit chief, which would have been used to store sacred crests of the clan.

A carved wooden panel from the interior of a house.

ravens are particularly beautiful. To the makers, the objects were spiritually powerful as well.

They used red and yellow cedar, yew, alder, maple, and Sitka spruce. Originally, their tools were of stone, shell, or beavers' teeth. When they began to trade with the Russians and Europeans, they received metal tools, but they still employed them in

When a Plains Indian mother was in labor, the father sang special songs and chants to help make the birth easier.

the traditional ways. Sometimes, the wood was painted as well as carved.

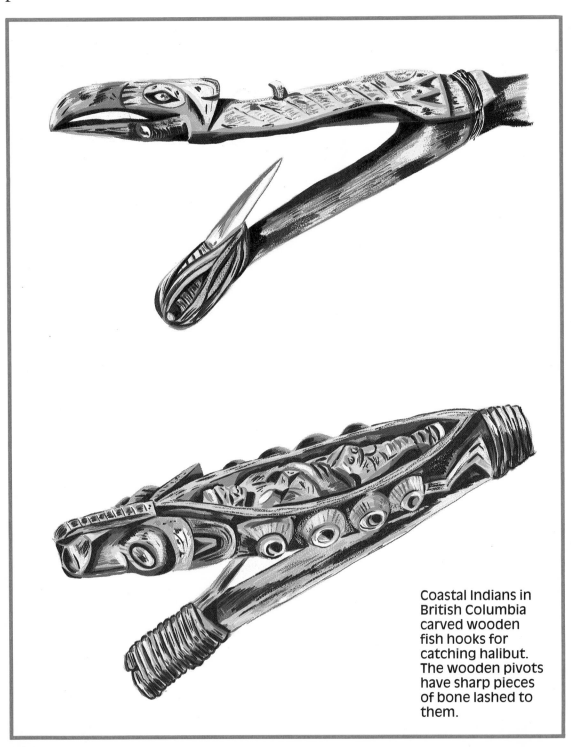

Coastal Indians in British Columbia carved wooden fish hooks for catching halibut. The wooden pivots have sharp pieces of bone lashed to them.

In 1958, the Province of British Columbia presented a carved wooden totem pole to Queen Elizabeth II. It now stands in Windsor Great Park, near London. It was made by Mungo Martin, a Kwakiutl chief.

Totem poles

Perhaps the best know examples of the woodcarvers' art are the huge carved and painted totem poles standing at the entrances of houses of the Pacific Coast tribes. Especially impressive are those made by the Tsimshian and Haida of the mainland and the Kwakiutl on Vancouver Island. Strangely enough, despite their name and the fact that Indian art was usually religious in intent, totem poles have nothing to do with the spiritual totems of their owners. They are a mixture of status symbol and family crest.

The Bella Coola tribe of the Northwest Coast enacted a drama in the spring which told the story of the rebirth of nature each year. There were actors playing the parts of trees and shrubs of the locality, the South Wind, and Mother Nature. Mother Nature sat behind the fire and gave birth, with the help of two midwives, to the willow, the gooseberry, the nettlegrass, and all the other plants in the order in which they actually sprout in the spring. Each plant was played by a member of the tribe, who danced around the fire.

Left: Tlingit totem poles. The one on the left has wolves at the top and bottom. On the top of the one on the right-hand side is a raven with a circle representing the sun around his face At the bottom is a frog.

Right: Totems at Wrangell, Alaska, in front of a modern two-story wooden house, photographed in 1883.

Peace pipes

The smoking of tobacco was a part of ancient Indian ritual. Stone pipes at least four thousand years old have been found in graves in the Eastern Woodlands. Pipes were smoked to seal a bargain or peace treaty. They were carried by a war chief to give him supernatural power in battle. On the Plains, a pipe was a symbol of authority. Sometimes, a pipe and tomahawk were combined in one article.

Pipes were made from wood, stone, argillite, and catlinite. Argillite, a kind of black slate, is found only on the Queen Charlotte Islands, the home of the Haida tribe. They also used it to make tiny totem

A selection of carved peace pipes and a tool for cleaning them. The tobacco pouch and pipe cover are decorated with beads and embroidery.

Tribes who lived around the Great Lakes in Minnesota, Wisconsin, Michigan, and Ontario made highly decorated pipes covered with beads, feathers, ribbons, and carvings. They valued these pipes so highly that the French called the tribe the "Calumet People," from the word "chalumeau," which is French for "pipe."

A Jesuit missionary, Father de Smet, wrote about the importance of their pipes to these people.

"On all great occasions, in their religious and political ceremonies, and at their great feasts, the calumet presides. The savages send its first fruits, or first puffs, to the Great Wakonda, or Master of Life, to the Sun which gives them light, and to the Earth and Water by which they are nourished; then they direct a puff to each part of the compass, begging of heaven and all the elements for favorable winds."

Haida man carving a totem pole.

poles and human figures to sell to Europeans. The Hopewell people, who were living in what is now Ohio in 200 A.D., carved beautiful pipes from stone in the shapes of animals.

Catlinite is a mineral, red or gray in color, named after the nineteenth century painter of Indians, George Catlin. Also known as pipestone, it was mined mainly from a quarry in Minnesota in what is now Pipestone National Park. The site did not belong to any particular tribe, but was available to all. When catlinite is first taken from the ground, it is fairly soft and easy to work; it hardens after exposure to the air. Catlinite pipe bowls were fitted to carved wooden stems.

Bone carvings

The shamans of the Northwest Coast tribes had amulets carved from bone, horn, bears' teeth, and ivory. They wore them as necklaces or sewn to their clothes. Sometimes, the carvings were inlaid with shells. They represented spirits. The Tlingits used shin bones of deer or elks to carve "soul catchers." It was believed that the shamans could use them to recapture the soul flying away from a man and make it return to his body.

Sculpture and pottery

In Tennessee and Oklahoma, ancient figurines,

Articles which combined a pipe with a tomahawk were manufactured in Birmingham, England, exported, and sold to the Indians. They then used them to kill their white enemies!

This little figure
carved from a
bear's fang was
possibly a
shaman's amulet.

made of pottery by Indian peoples such as the Hopewell, have been found. In general, the making of large sculptures does not seem to have been an art form which particularly appealed to native North Americans. Some modern Indians of the Southwest are, however, experimenting with it. The Indians' skills were traditionally demonstrated in their stone carvings of small animal and human figures on their pipes and bowls.

The women showed artistic ability and a sense of design in the making and decorating of pots for cooking, holding water, and other domestic uses.

A pot with painted geometric decoration.

Pueblo potters with examples of geometric and animal designs on their pots.

The Mississippi Mound Builders, who lived along the banks of the river in the first and second centuries A.D., made attractive pottery figures, pipes, jars, and bottles. A famous pipe shows a warrior wearing armor cutting off the head of an enemy. Some of their bottles were joined in pairs like Siamese twins.

The earliest North American Indian pottery dates from 200 B.C. It was made by the people of the Mogollon culture of the southwest, and the knowledge of how to make it came from Mexico.

The Indians did not use a pottery wheel. They had two main methods of working with clay. In the west and southwest, they made "sausages" of clay mixed with grit, coiled them around, one on top of another, and smoothed the pot inside and out with a piece of gourd. This method is still used in the Pueblos today. The peoples of the south and southeast preferred to slap clay on, or into, an existing pot which served as a mold. Decoration is added before firing, either by the use of mineral slips and glazes such as kaolin, or by engraving the surface with a sharp object, or by pressing with the thumbs and fingers. The pots are fired in a pile of burning dung which burns evenly. Where coal is locally available, as among the Hopi, it is used.

Sometimes, the pots are painted after firing, using vegetable and mineral dyes applied with a chewed yucca leaf. The traditional designs are geometric, animal, and human forms. The work of comparatively modern Indian potters, such as Maria and Julian Martinez of the San Ildefonso Pueblo, is much admired and in demand. Their work has designs in mat black applied to a shiny black surface, which is the result of firing for a long time with the smoke sealed in. The Hopi and the Maricopa tribes also make excellent pots. The Maricopa specialize in high-necked jars in a bright red color.

Painting

There are also respected modern watercolorists who are continuing the traditions of their ancestors. Most come from the southwest and have been encouraged by white Americans. In Santa Fe, soon after World War I, a group of American artists made

An oil painting on canvas with wood entitled *Papa Would Like You* by the Indian artist Alvin Eli Amason. He says, "I like this one because of the youth and hope it expresses."

a determined effort to make Indian art better known and appreciated. Later, in 1923, the Indian Art Fund provided funds for exhibitions of Indian work. San Ildefonso is a center for painting as well as pottery, although it has a population of only about three hundred. The enthusiasm spread to the neighboring Navajo, Apache, Hopi, Kiowa, and Sioux tribes, who have all produced talented painters.

Modern Indian artists use their knowledge of traditional ideas and designs. They combine them with an increasing understanding of the way in which the white men's drawing uses perspective. This is an attempt to portray realistically objects which have length, width, and depth on a piece of paper which has only length and width. Traditionally, the Indians did not paint pictures to hang on a wall, but painted the objects they used, from hats and shields to tepees, and they painted themselves. Originally, their paints were made from grinding up colored clays and minerals or by boiling the leaves or roots of various plants to make natural dyes. Black came from charcoal, red and yellow from ocher, green from copper ore, and white from a special clay called kaolin. When they began to trade with the white men, they acquired chemically produced paints which are generally brighter in hue.

The Plains Indians painted scenes such as buffalo hunts and battles on their tepees and robes. They used wedge-shaped pieces of bone instead of brushes. The sharp edges were used for drawing lines and the flat surface for filling in blocks of color. The paint was made to stick by mixing it with grease, water, or the juice from the leaves of the prickly pear cactus. Like some of the tribes of British Columbia, including the Kutenai and the Interior Salish, the people of the Plains painted on rocks their interpretations of visions which they had seen.

The Shaman Beckons, a woodcut produced in 1971 by the Indian artist Joseph E. Senungetuk.

Opposite: Plains Indians used bones and pots of paint to decorate hide for clothes and tepees. This painting emphasizes the importance of the horse to them.

Crescencio Martinez was one of the first Indians to experiment with painting in watercolors. He produced a great deal of highly regarded work in about 1910, but in 1918 he died from Spanish flu. He lived in San Ildefonso Pueblo and was the brother-in-law of Maria Martinez, the potter. His example encouraged others of the Pueblo to paint, and it became a well known center for Indian art.

The Northwest Coast tribes added painted decoration to their carving and basketry. They ground the paint on stone palettes. The paints were mixed with chewed-up salmon eggs and cedar bark, so that the design would adhere and not rub off. The peoples of the southwest decorated their pottery with painted designs. Geometric patterns were often used on pots and baskets.

Painting with a stick on a hat made of woven split spruce roots.

A form of painting in which the Navajo specialize is sand painting. This art is practiced by the medicine men and is part of a deeply religious healing cere-

Some of the oldest examples of Indian art are petroglyphs, which can be found on rocks all over North America. They are drawings, shapes, and symbols scratched into rocks. Some of them may have been done by young Indians sent out on a vision quest, or they may commemorate important events and treaties.

mony. The sick person sits on the ground, and the medicine man creates a special design around him by trickling different colored sands, powdered plants, cornmeal, and pollen through his fingers. It is believed that the illness is absorbed into the paintings. At sunset, the painting is destroyed, and the illness disappears with it. The designs are traditional and are retained only in the memories of the medicine men. They often contain a rainbow, which is the symbol of rain and fertility.

Etching

The etching of designs on metal and shell is an ancient Indian skill. The Hohokam people, who lived in Arizona from about 1,000 B.C., knew how to scratch a design through a coating of wax and then fix it with the acid juice of the giant cactus. The Mississippi Mound Builders who lived at Cahokia, Missouri, in 1,200 A.D. also etched shells. Their designs included eagles, vultures, and serpents and were influenced by Mexican ideas. Many of them were concerned with death, and a symbolic "weeping eye" is a common motif in their art.

Metalwork

Although the Indians never developed the techniques of smelting or casting metal and the making of iron tools and utensils, they did mine and

A band of the Chipewyan tribe who live in the subarctic region are called the Yellowknifes. This name comes from the copper which they used to make their tools and weapons.

work local copper and silver. Indians around Lake Superior knew in 5,000 B.C. that when copper became brittle through too much hammering, it could be made malleable again by heating it in a fire. These people of the Old Copper Culture of Wisconsin, Minnesota, and Michigan made arrowheads, spearheads, knives, and axes.

Copper was beaten into sheets by the Hopewell

Zuni blacksmiths at work in their forge.

41

people, who were living in Illinois in about 200 A.D. From these sheets, they carved silhouettes of human heads and bird talons. The Hopewells also used copper to make axes, awls, ear studs, and fish hooks. The Mississippi Mound Builders cut out and embossed sheets of copper. The Northwest Coast tribes made huge shields of copper. They were highly valued as a sign of the great wealth of the owner. Across the Plains and among the people of the Lakes and the Iroquois, the skill of making buttons, buckles, and jewelry spread from the eighteenth century European explorers. It is believed that a Navajo man called Atsidi Sani, ("Old Smith") learned the knowledge of how to work in silver from a Mexican craftsman in about 1868. He taught his sons, and the knowledge spread. The Navajo used to melt down U.S. and Mexican coins, but they now buy raw silver imported from Mexico, Asia, and the Middle East. The silver is either cast from molds of clay or sandstone, or it is hammered and filed. Some pieces may require a combination of both methods.

At first, the Navajo made buckles and buttons. Buttons used to be made by hammering coins into a hemispherical shape. Soldering two together formed a bead. Tiny bells were made by attaching clappers to them; women used to wear them on their sashes to warn their sons-in-law when they were coming. "Conchas" are large oval disks worn on belts, and "ketohs" are heavy wristguards which protect the wearer from the string of a bow as the arrow is released.

Jewelry

There are signs of the influence of Eastern countries such as Morocco in the crescent pendants called "najahe." This influence probably came from the

Peshlakai, or Slender Silvermaker, a famous Navajo silversmith, photographed about 1885. Both the crescent-shaped pendant and the circular medallions are typical Navajo designs.

Spanish explorers, since the Moors of Morocco once ruled the part of Spain now known as Andalusia. What the Navajo call a squash-blossom design was probably originally a Spanish pomegranate.

The Indians loved wearing beads and silver jewelry.

From about 1880, Navajo silversmiths began to use turquoise in a setting of silver for rings, bracelets, necklaces, and earrings. A clear blue stone is more highly valued than one which is greenish and veined. Some of the stone is found locally; the rest is imported from Pueblo villages and countries as distant as Iran and China. Navajo jewelry is very popular outside the tribe, but is is not made just for tourists. The Navajos wear and treasure it themselves as well. Cheap copies of Navajo jewelry are mass produced in Japan, Taiwan, and Los Angeles.

There are also skilled jewelers among the Zuni

and the Hopi, neighbors of the Navajo. Zuni designs tend to be smaller and more delicate than Navajo work, and they use a wider variety of stones. Black jet, pink coral, creamy pearls and abalone shells, and deep red garnet, as well as turquoise, are used to make mosaics in the shapes of birds, butterflies, and other creatures. In their use of shells for jewelry, the Zuni maintain a tradition which stretches back to the Hohokam, who imported shells from California. The Hopi tend not to use stones, but they engrave their work.

Weaving

Another craft at which the Navajo excel is weaving. They originally learned the skill from the Pueblos in about 1700. Among the Pueblo peoples, the men usually weave in the kivas, the sacred meeting houses of various secret societies. They make woolen blankets in striped patterns, as well as some in black and white plaid. Weaving in cotton is also an ancient craft of the area.

Among the Navajo, however, weaving is generally done by the women; the men are usually the silversmiths. They use a vertical loom and weave out-doors. The woman kneels on the ground and

White hairs grow under the throat, in the mane, and on the rump of moose and caribou. Iroquois and Huron women of the Northeastern Woodlands dyed them and used them decoratively in their weaving. The hairs were folded around the weft threads to produce an embroidered effect.

begins to weave from the bottom of the frame. She passes the weft threads through the warp using her fingers and a small rod instead of a shuttle. To make the weaving firm, the weft is pushed down with a bar of wood.

Threads were traditionally made from vegetable fiber and animal hair and later cotton. Now the weavers spin and weave wool from the herds of sheep which they own. The wool is sheared, carded

An intricate geometric design for a woven tunic.

Right: A Chilkat shirt now in the National Museum of Canada, Ottawa.

with a toothed instrument to untangle the fibers, washed in suds from the yucca plant, and spun on a wooden spindle. The wool may need to be spun as many as six times to produce yarn which is fine and strong enough. The yarn is used to make rugs and blankets.

The designs are generally brightly colored patterns made from geometric shapes, stripes, and zigzag lines. In the old days, the dyes came from vegetables and minerals mixed with alum, urine, or ashes to make them stay fast in the wool. In about 1800, Spanish traders introduced red flannel. The Navajo loved this color and unraveled the fabrics to incorporate the threads into their own weaving. Some blankets which were very tightly woven with finely spun yarn are said to have been waterproof. They were used for clothing and bedding and as saddlecloths. Because Navajo blankets are very time-consuming to make, they are expensive, and today most of them are exported. The Indians themselves use blankets woven by machine.

Hand weaving has been done by the Indians since

The extinct Natchez tribe lived in what is now Mississippi until the seventeenth century. Their beds were made from woven reed mats on a framework of poles which was supported by four poles at the corners. They also used mats, up to six feet long and four feet wide, to line the walls of their mud houses. The mats had geometrical designs woven into them. Clothes were woven from the fibers of mulberry bark, nettle, and the hair of buffalo and oppossum.

prehistoric times. The Adena and Hopewell peoples made textiles without looms. The Chilkat of the Northwest Coast made treasured blankets which were used on ceremonial occasions. To make the blankets strong, they used shredded cedar bark for the warp threads, which hung down from a single bar. Mountain goat wool, dyed black, white, yellow, and blue-green, was woven through the warp with the fingers. The designs often included borders and animal patterns. The blankets were usually six feet long; they were two feet wide at the ends and wider in the middle. There was thick fringe around three of the edges.

The Salish of northern California and the North-west Coast wove the hair from specially-bred dogs, as well as goat and sheep wool. They wove on looms and made blankets with square patterns in red, blue, black, and white. The Hopi were also good at weaving.

Basketry

The making of baskets is a craft closely related to the weaving of cloth. Many North American tribes showed great skill and ingenuity in their use of local materials to produce a variety of useful nets and baskets of every shape and size. Baskets were used for storing, carrying, and cooking food. They could be woven so tightly that they were watertight. Baskets were even used for washing and for dying clothes. Cradles for babies, mats and trays, bowls and sieves, lobster pots, hats, chests, and canisters up to six feet tall for storing grain were just some of the everyday objects which were woven from plant materials. The plants which were used included rushes and grasses such as bear grass, buffalo grass, and sweet grass; the roots and bark of trees including oak, cedar, and spruce; yucca leaves and twigs from the willow and

Top: A basketmaker from the Karok tribe. The baby is resting on a woven cradleboard.

Bottom: A woman of the Papago tribe kneels outside her stick and wattle home making baskets.

other trees. The Indians of each region used what was available in their area. Most plants, if they were suitably treated by soaking or steaming, could be used for weaving something.

Other materials, such as feathers, shells, buckskin fringes, bells, beads, and porcupine quills, were used to decorate baskets. These adornments were applied particularly to baskets used for ceremonies such as weddings and funerals and those which were made to be given as gifts. Designs were also incorporated by weaving in contrasting dyed fibers or by painting the finished object. When feathers were woven in with the fibers, a very soft effect, almost like velvet, was created.

The people of the desert regions in the west first began making baskets at least ten thousand years ago. They made coiled and twined baskets, hunting traps, and sandals. The Apache, Navajo, Pima, and Papago peoples of the southwest still make beautiful baskets, although today they are more often made to sell than for home use. As with their hand-woven blankets, it is cheaper to buy mass-produced goods.

Many Americans attend classes to learn the ancient skills from today's native Americans.

Quillwork, beads, and embroidery

The quills of the wild porcupine were used by Indian women for the embroidered decoration of clothes, bags, and quivers. Northeastern Woodland tribes such as the Micmac and the Ojibwa, the Iroquois further south, the Prairie tribes, and those of the Northwest Coast all employed this art very skillfully. The quills vary in length, thickness, and color according to which part of the porcupine's body they come from. The white ones can be dyed.

To use them, the women first moistened and then flattened them using either a bone plate or their

A shirt, moccasin, belt, rifle holster, and knife pouch are all decorated with beads.

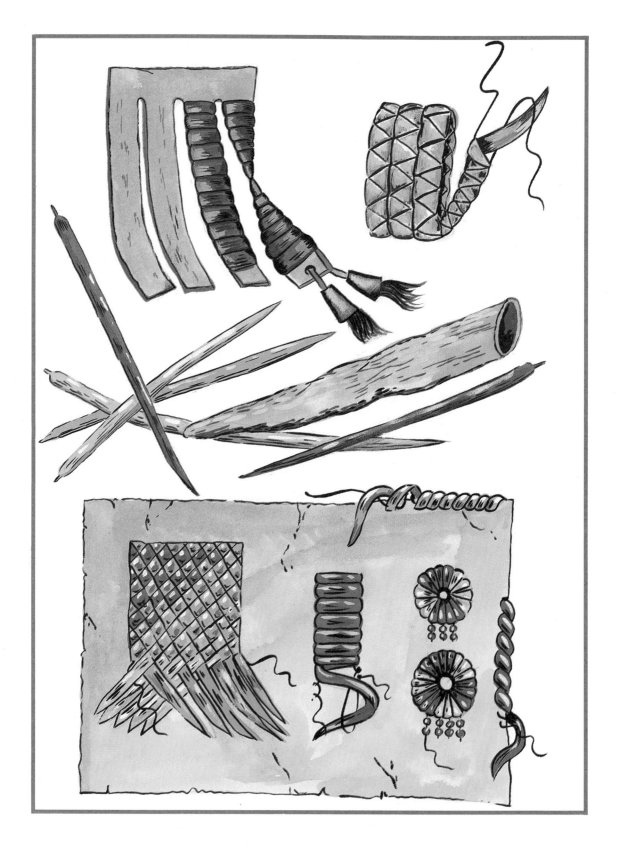

fingers. Then the quills were ready to be sewn onto fabric using sinew as thread. Alternatively, they were woven into bands, which were then sewn onto a garment or bag. This method had an extra advantage: the decoration could be removed when the garment was worn out and re-used on something else. Cree and Athabaskan women were experts at this art, and it was also practiced among the tribes of the Plains.

Beads were popular items for the decoration of clothes and containers, and as they became readily available, they tended to replace quillwork. At first, the Indians made their own beads by cutting, drilling, and polishing shells and stones. When the Europeans introduced imported glass beads in the sixteenth and seventeenth centuries, the Indians were

Mars-che-coodo, or White Man Runs Him, of the Crow tribe was one of General Custer's scouts. This photograph of 1910 shows him wearing many beads as well as face paint.

A simple loom used by some Pueblos and Navajos has the warp threads attached from a belt around the weaver's waist to a house pole or tree. It is used to produce belts. Particularly popular ones are red and green with white cotton designs, which are produced by Navajo women.

very attracted by them and used them enthusiastically, mainly in necklaces because they were large.

Many of these beads, which were individually made by glass blowers, are beautiful and are now collectors' items. Some had names, such as the Padre Bead, the Sun Bead, and the Chevron Bead. Turquoise beads from Czechoslovakia were popular among the Navajo in the 1920s. When smaller machine-made beads became easy to obtain, the Indians used them to decorate fabric and skins. The Kutenai decorated their cradles with them. On the Plains, a stitch called lazystitch was used, so called because several beads in a row were sewn on with one stitch. Beads were also incorporated into weaving. Saddles and harnesses were brightly decorated with beads as well.

The Indians take a pride in their traditional skills, and much of their work is prized by tourists from many parts of the world. In the modern world, everyday objects are cheaply produced and carelessly tossed aside when they wear out, break, or go out of fashion. Yet there is still a market for well-designed, well-made and attractively decorated articles such as those which native Americans continue to make today. They offer an alternative way of valuing things and using time.

Glossary

abstract impression   the idea of the feelings produced by an object or event

alum   a sulfate of aluminum and potassium

anthropology   the study of the societies and customs of mankind

amulet   something worn as a charm against evil spirits

cast   to shape things from metal which is heated until it melts

ceremony   a special occasion, often of religious importance, which includes traditional chants, songs, speeches, or actions

charcoal   the blackened remains of partly burned wood or bones

embossed   carved so that the design stands up from the surface of the object

essence   the things about a person, animal, or object which make it unique and individual

ethnography   scientific study of the races of men

geometric   shapes made of straight lines and circles

hemisphere   half of a ball shape

kaolin   fine, white clay

kachinas   ancestral spirits

malleable   able to be hammered or pressed into shape without breaking

Moors   Moslem people from northwest Africa

mosaic   a pattern or picture made from tiny pieces of stone or glass joined together

motif a feature of a design or pattern

ocher a clay from which yellow and brown paints can be made

ore metal and minerals in their natural state as they are mined from the ground

perspective a technique used in drawing three dimensional objects. Lines which are parallel in reality are drawn so that they come to a point in a picture

petroglyphs ancient rock carvings

ritual actions carried out in a special way, usually for a religious purpose

shaman medicine man, priest

silhouette the blocked-in outline of a shape or figure

sinew tough tissue which joins muscles to bones

slip clay which is finely ground and mixed with water for covering or making patterns on pottery

smelting melting ore to extract metal

solder to join edges of metal, often by welding another softer metal between them

symbolic representing an idea with an object. The Indians used a picture of an eye weeping to symbolize the idea of death and the sorrow and grief which it brings

textile woven fabric

totem the emblem representing the spirit of an animal or object which a band, clan, or tribe regard as their spiritual guardian

vertical upright

Table of Tribes
This list shows some of the most important Indian tribes of North America, the regions in which they lived and the languages spoken.

FAR NORTH
Algonquin; Macro-Algonkian
Beaver; Na-Dene
Beothuk; Language group unknown
Carrier; Na-Dene
Chilcotin; Na-Dene
Chipewyan; Na-Dene
Cree; Macro-Algonkian
Dogrib; Na-Dene
Hare; Na-Dene
Kaska; Na-Dene
Koyukon; Na-Dene
Kutchin; Na-Dene
Micmac; Macro-Algonkian
Montagnais; Macro-Algonkian
Naskapi; Macro-Algonkian
Ottawa; Macro-Algonkian
Sarsi; Na-Dene
Slave; Na-Dene
Tanaina; Na-Dene
Tutchone; Na-Dene
Yellowknife; Na-Dene

NORTHWEST COAST
Bella Coola; Language group unknown
Chilkat; Na-Dene
Chinook; Penutian
Coast Salish; Language group unknown
Haida; Na-Dene
Klikitat; Penutian
Kwakiutl; Language group unknown
Nootka; Language group unknown
Quileute; Language group unknown
Quinault; Language group unknown
Tlingit; Na-Dene
Tsimshian; Penutian

CALIFORNIA-INTERMOUNTAIN
Bannock; Aztec-Tanoan
Cayuse; Penutian
Chumash; Hokan
Diegueño; Hokan
Flathead; Language group unknown
Gabrielino; Aztec-Tanoan
Gosiute; Aztec-Tanoan
Hupa; Na-Dene
Interior Salish; Language group unknown

Karok; Hokan
Klamath; Penutian
Kutenai; Language group unknown
Maidu; Penutian
Modoc; Penutian
Mohave; Hokan
Nez Percé; Penutian
Paiute; Aztec-Tanoan
Pomo; Hokan
Shoshoni; Aztec-Tanoan
Ute; Aztec-Tanoan
Wintun; Penutian

SOUTHWEST
Apache; Na-Dene
Cochimi; Hokan
Havasupai; Hokan
Maricopa; Hokan
Navajo; Na-Dene
Papago; Aztec-Tanoan
Pima; Aztec-Tanoan
Pueblo:
   Acoma; Language group unknown
   Hopi; Aztec-Tanoan
   Laguna; Language group unknown
   San Ildefonso; Aztec-Tanoan
   Taos; Aztec-Tanoan
   Zia; Language group unknown
Zuñi; Language group unknown
Waiguri; Hokan
Yaqui; Aztec-Tanoan
Yuma; Hokan

PLAINS
Arapaho; Macro-Algonkian
Arikara; Macro-Siouan
Assiniboin; Macro-Siouan
Atakapa; Macro-Algonkian
Blackfeet:
   Blood; Macro-Algonkian
   Piegan; Macro-Algonkian
Caddo; Macro-Siouan
Cheyenne; Macro-Algonkian
Comanche: Aztec-Tanoan
Crow; Macro-Siouan
Gros Ventre; Macro-Algonkian
Hidatsa; Macro-Siouan

Iowa; Macro-Siouan
Kansa; Macro-Siouan
Karankawa; Language group
  unknown
Kiowa; Aztec-Tanoan
Mandan; Macro-Siouan
Missouri; Macro-Siouan
Omaha; Macro-Siouan
Osage; Macro-Siouan
Pawnee; Macro-Siouan
Ponca; Macro-Siouan
Quapaw; Macro-Siouan
Sioux; (Dakotah):
  Oglala; Macro-Siouan
  Santee; Macro-Siouan
  Sisseton; Macro-Siouan
  Teton; Macro-Siouan
  Yankton; Macro-Siouan
Wichita; Macro-Siouan

EASTERN WOODLANDS
Abnaki; Northeast; Macro-Algonkian
Calusa; Southeast; Macro-Siouan
Cherokee; Southeast; Macro-Siouan
Chickasaw; Southeast; Macro-Algonkian
Chippewa; Northeast & Far North;
  Macro-Algonkian
Chitimacha; Southeast; Macro-Algonkian

Choctaw; Southeast; Macro-Algonkian
Conestoga; Northeast; Macro-Siouan
Creek; Southeast; Macro-Algonkian
Delaware (Lenape); Northeast;
  Macro-Algonkian
Huron; Northeast; Macro-Siouan
Illinois; Northeast; Macro-Algonkian
Iroquois; Northeast; Macro-Siouan
Kickapoo; Northeast; Macro-Algonkian
Malecite; Northeast; Macro-Algonkian
Massachusetts; Northeast;
  Macro-Algonkian
Menominee; Northeast; Macro-Algonkian
Miami; Northeast; Macro-Algonkian
Missisauga; Northeast; Macro-Algonkian
Mohican; Northeast; Macro-Algonkian
Natchez; Southeast; Macro-Algonkian
Potawatomi; Northeast; Macro Algonkian
Powhatan; Southeast; Macro-Algonkian
Sauk; Northeast; Macro-Algonkian
Seminole;Southeast; Macro-Algonkian
Shawnee; Southeast; Macro-Algonkian
Timucua; Southeast; Language group
  unknown
Tuscarora; Southeast; Macro-Siouan
Wampanoag; Northeast; Macro-Algonkian
Winnebago; Northeast; Macro-Siouan

Tribal Areas

THE FAR NORTH AREA

Algonquin	Dogrib	Naskapi
Beaver	Hare	Ottawa
Beothuk	Kaska	Sarsi
Carrier	Koyukon	Slave
Chilcotin	Kutchin	Tanaina
Chipewyan	Micmac	Tutchone
Cree	Montagnais	Yellowknife

THE NORTHWEST COAST AREA

Chinook
Haida
Klikitat
Kwakiutl
Nootka
Quileute
Quinault
Tlingit
Tsimshian

CALIFORNIA-INTERMOUNTAIN

Bannock	Karok	Mohave
Cayuse	Klamath	Nez Percé
Chumash	Kutenai	Paiute
Flathead	Luiseno	Pomo
Gosiute	Maidu	Shoshoni
Hupa	Modoc	Ute
		Wintun

THE SOUTHWEST AREA

Apache	Laguna
Cochimi	San Ildefonso
Navajo	Taos
Papago	Zia
Pima	Zuñi
Pueblo:	Waiguri
Acoma	Yaqui
Hopi	Yuma

THE PLAINS AREA

Arapaho	Crow	Pawnee
Arikara	Gros Ventre	Ponca
Assiniboin	Hidatsa	Quapaw
Atakapa	Iowa	Sioux:
Blackfeet:	Kansa	Oglala
Blood	Karankawa	Santee
Plegan	Klowa	Sisseton
Caddo	Mandan	Teton
Cheyenne	Omaha	Yankton
Comanche	Osaga	Wichita

THE EASTERN WOODLANDS AREA

NORTHEAST

Abnaki		
Chippewa	Massachusetts	
Delaware	Menominee	
Erie	Miami	
Fox	Mohegan	
Huron	Narraganset	Chitimacha
Illinois	Potawatomi	Choctaw
Iroquois:	Sauk	Creek
Cayuga	Susquehanna	Natchez
Mohawk	Wampanoag	Powhatan
Onondaga	Winnebago	Seminole
Oneida		Shawnee
Seneca	SOUTHEAST	Timucua
Kickapoo	Calusa	Tuscarora
Mahican	Cherokee	Yamasee
Malecite	Chickasaw	Yuchi

The major linguistic areas

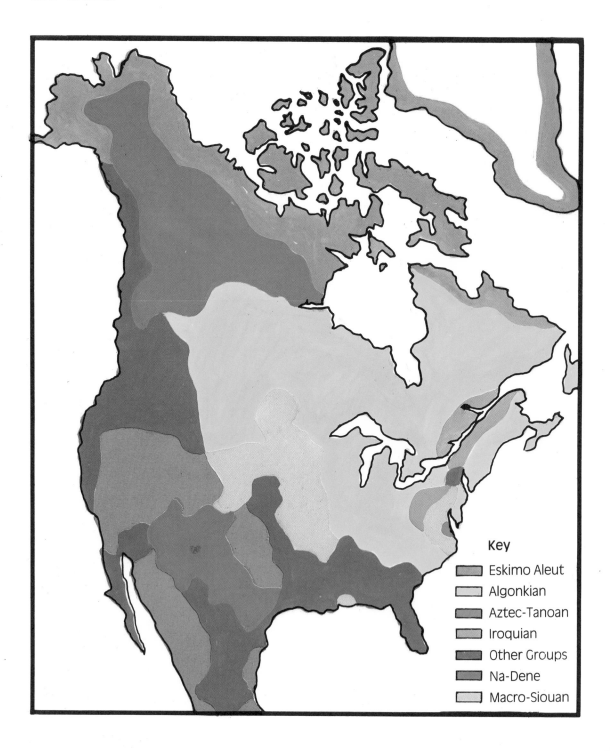

Key

Eskimo Aleut
Algonkian
Aztec-Tanoan
Iroquian
Other Groups
Na-Dene
Macro-Siouan

Index

Index of tribes

Numbers in *italics* refer to
illustrations.